POETRY WITH A FLOE

Du-En Rennie Foster Sr.

POETRY WITH A FLOE

iUniverse books may be ordered through booksellers or by contacting:

iUniverse
1663 Liberty Drive
Bloomington, IN 47403
www.iuniverse.com
844-349-9409

Because of the dynamic nature of the Internet, any web addresses or links contained in
this book may have changed since publication and may no longer be valid. The views
expressed in this work are solely those of the author and do not necessarily reflect the
views of the publisher, and the publisher hereby disclaims any responsibility for them.

Any people depicted in stock imagery provided by Getty Images are
models, and such images are being used for illustrative purposes only.
Certain stock imagery © Getty Images.

ISBN: 978-1-6632-2587-0 (sc)
ISBN: 978-1-6632-2586-3 (e)

Library of Congress Control Number: 2021916041

Print information available on the last page.

iUniverse rev. date: 08/06/2021

CONTENTS

ACKNOWLEDGEMENTS

1. I would like to thank God for giving me the ability to put words into a poetry with a floe form.
2. I would like to thank my father R.I.P Mr. Alfred P. Foster for telling me to make enough money to own your own home 1 day, and pick up that penny 100 pennies equals a dollar. I still pick up pennies to this very day.
3. I like to thank Ms. Dorothy M. Smith Foster my mother for making sure that I have food, clothing and shelter.
4. I would like to thank my sister Ms. Shelly Smith for all the Numerous things she's done for me.
5. I would like to thank my brother Hershlle Bolden Jr. for keeping me on track as much as possible.

6. I would like to thank my sister Ms. Grace Foster Hardie for always teaching me the facts of life of woman also a good story about Saint Thomas.

7. I would like to thank my sister Ms. Thomas Dorothy for taking the time out to make every family function.

8. I would like to thank my brother Mr. VON-AL M. Foster Sr. for always Supporting me in everything I do Positive, and for always having my back in every form, shape and fashion.

9. I would like to thank Ms. Stephanie Parks for being our 6 adult children mother, and a good friend to me from 1982 to Present.

10. I like to thank my 6 adult children, and 10 Grandchildren. My adult children as followed first # 1 R.I.P Du-En Rennie Foster Jr., Theresa E. Foster, La- Mel V. Foster, La- Tonya Foster, Felicia Foster, and Jessica Parks.

11. I would like to thank my friend Nicola, and her family.

12. I would like to thank my friend Keith, and his family.

13. I would like to thank Siobhan, and her family.

14. I would like to thank my friend Urban and his family.

15. I like to thank my kids Grandmother, Ms. Shirley White.

16. I would like to thank Lady Willa Gregory, and Daughter: Sharilynn Erika Lichtensteiger, Mr. Kendall C. McCray (K.C), Mr. Vaughn Q. Keith, and family of Catherine Yvonne Keith, for being there for me.

17. Also our PET our dog Ying- Yang RIP.

18. I would like to thank my Cousin Mr. Lenny Mixson R.I.P and my Aunt Ms. Elizabeth Mixson aka Aunt Lizzie R.I.P ,.and my Cousin Mr. Vaughn Mixson. Also all of the rest of my family, and friends.

19. LAST and NOT LEAST MY FIANCÉE CATHERINE YVONNE KEITH AKA TIGER🐱 CAT😺 FOR ALL HER SUPPORT.

I L💔VE YOU
EVERYONE.▦

TIGER CAT THE MOST MAGNIFICENT

Dedicated Love floetry poem.

TIGER CAT you shine like a diamond that just came out of a volcano when it was extremely hot which makes Coal the most expensive rock, and like a archeologists Scientist I want to cover every spot your grace is like a musical wind up jewelry box, and let me remind you, it was made out of crystal a pandora was the first name it was issued. TIGER CAT also like a carousel you're beautiful you don't have to improve your game play, because you don't play NO GAMES. TIGER CAT your whole body definition are composed collectively like love FLOETRY to infinity I love thee early. TIGER CAT your beautiful structure is at it's purest forms, you're the elements that produce the sweet honey that's in the hexagons of a bee's honey comb. TIGER CAT you also got a natural fragrance like flowers that are already known. We would be in our relationship using our inner soul's to develop a NO EVALUATION ZONE on love, and love making, and on good friendship, and good feelings, that's the measurements of what you're mind frame would be in. THREE HUNDRED AND SIXTY DEGREES as it spins. TIGER CAT are you thinking of a different period when the cellphone was already invented, look at Get Smart, Inspector Gadget, the Vis - O - phone on the Jetsons, Face Time, Dick Tracy with the watch, TIGER CAT NOW your getting it, the Spa, the Roses, and the Chocolates. TIGER CAT I will love you like the feelings you got when you thought that Santa Claus was filling up your Christmas Stockings. TIGER CAT I'm the electricity that will get the Energizer bunny started. TIGER CAT I won't leave you even if we were dearly departed. I'm in need of a lot of subscribers mostly, Singers, Rappers, and POET'S, and those with Knowledge. TIGER CAT you're a beautiful woman that can take on any Jeopardy game show challenge. TIGER CAT if you was on an Island what would you eat? That question will be the hardest because TIGER CAT you was never marooned you own your own Cottage, like a Mansion the decorations are created from your own decorative knowledge. TIGER CAT it was created on the blueprints right when you first started that's how your BEAUTY, and your HEART is tailor made from the start Ms. I love TIGER CAT that's why I will always send you a THREE HUNDRED AND SIXTY DEGREES of a KISS peace my TIGER CAT the most magnificent. PEACE.

. . . .

By Du-En Rennie Foster Sr.

aka floetry poet

3 ☐6 ☐0 ☐™ LY☺☺☺☺✍

REBORN YOU
The Spoken Word.

I have the tools you need that would make you irresistible.
I've been doing this since New York City have been using
bambu'. If you clap your hands twice they're all will be
dancing in Egyptian for you. I've already crowned you
KING and QUEEN you were born Royal I'm your Steet
father that's why I adore you and, to the dumb, dedf
and blind, this is definitely for you. At this present time
your signnal bars are so, low you should use a homing
pigeon. Because that's how long it takes before your
instant messaging get the reaching Morse code is more
in your Division, I can hand sign if you can't listen,
or get a TTY George Jetson Vis-O-phone connection.
I'm that mad scientist in the kitchen with my teeth

glistiening, my hands spinning, and my back is hunched again, and laugh has that Hood Grin While preparing for that spectacular well-rounded life. Educating men, children and women, like a Native American Indian mending your organs from deep within, black coffee is the knowledge I'm bringing. I'm running a Seance is what I'm saying, I'm scribbling on your school desk with crayons. I must start from the beginnings. There's a lot of homie kins that can use my mending, and I'm wokeu, and I'm civilizing them while we are changing like chameleons, because all birds flock to-get-her great minds think together now spell them whatever, I know that was kind of clever, so bright it's like actingniting an old flash gunpowerd camera, the light so debonair you should have seen one, the Kodak camera with the round bulb flash son, then they came out with the square bulb one we shook this one while the immaculate one's develop like the sun. Instantermaic, digital, and now cellphoneone one's yes a phenomenal! PEACE.

. . . .

By Du-En Rennie Foster Sr.

aka floetry poet

3   ☐6   ☐0   ☐™   LY😊😊😊😊✍

ENLIGHTENING MANKIND
The Spoken Word.

You should see my thoughts they are extremely right like James Brown in the movie The Blues Brother's do- you- see- the- light? I'm that drug that can get your third eye nice. I'm sharp Smart like a Apple eye communication device I came up living the ghetto Wall Street life but BROOKLYN NEW YORK CITY, is mine a cast of thought of memories, and the streets is mine's by being a part of me, I'm from the District called KINGS COUNTY a region of dis also loyalty. I'm a Decepticon a Transformer I- can-not- be. Illusion IS like a part of magic from under my sleeves. I'm thinking on who's going to Bail out Wall Street? Soon you will see or not to see kids remembering this part of History. Your grand- grands will read about Obama, and Hillary in a hard book binder covering around 2024 it can be a WOMAN candidate presidency verses a WOMEN candidate presidency. What do you thinking gee? A eye or a thought, it's 2015 bee. Now I ain't doing any physic looking this is just how my mind be moving. Now what are you Du-En? That's my first name children. PEACE.

. . . .

By Du-En Rennie Foster Sr.

aka floetry poet

3 ⬜6 ⬜0 ⬜™   LY✊✊✊✊✍

DESIGN FOR TIGER CAT
Dedicated Love poem.

TIGER CAT now that your mine's I would handle you with great care, like the brand new mothers having their first child born everywhere. That first breath when you had said yeah! Something like a Mother's getting her kids out of Foster care, and from the father from the start that has always been there the father that give his virgin daughter alway in her Vail, and wedding wear. I respect you like my last sip of unseen air. I will love you as if you where helping me in a burning building as if we both has been in or around there, because I can't see how to go through the Smoky atmosphere. You're telling me the stire exit's are over there. You got my X and Y chromosome spreading rapidly, in a the circumference of 360 Degrees. Ms. your Love wone internatialy all around the globe completely. Your the model that teaches the modeles on how to be a model completely, on T.V. expertly.The ticket take praied is what I mean in your float smiling, and waving, and your not artifically flavored, like Duncan & Hines. Ma' for you I got that craving I'm full grown, and I like to have fun and fooling around Ma' I don't do that one. PEACE. By floetry poet 360 that would be me. I love you TIGER CAT. PEACE.

. . . .

By Du-En Rennie Foster Sr.
aka floetry poet

3   ☐6   ☐0   ☐TM   LYLY😁😁😁😁✍

THIS PROCESS IS KNOWN AS DROPPING LOVE SCIENCE

floetry Rap.

From the Old School to the new school both of them I'm going to use this is something you should get used to. You should be able to see this like you're watching Youtube. I'm getting out the Android to bring a whole new world to you I'm moving at 4G speed so get your Bluetooths. Like the red, and white blood cells once again I'm floeing right through you. Like Big Daddy Kane what you on dope or dog food? You should be like the Wii game swinging your arms as your body moves. I've been doing this since the days of Krush Groove, Technique Turn Tables are the tables that we use to use. Like this

CD turntables my voice has taking over uses too. Like the Casio watches are one of the first to go digital, and now they have a diamond G-Shock diamond watch for you, roll out the red carpet or whatever color carpet you choose. Now that there a complete temperature boil 212° Fahrenheit is that hot enough for you? Also 100° Celsius is the temperature of boil. This part is for the ladies I will always adore you I will never hurt you with great cruelty. Now your world is being delivered by me. That would be a complete introduction on how to live P.C.B witch stand for PERSONAL CHARACTER BUILDING having debative arguments no more we will be using. That would be off the air like the T.V. soap show all my children. Your simply marvellous 50/50 is what we will be using, unless I was deceased you won't say, all by my self I grew up all my children the recipe to 360 is what I'll be using keeping my mind on that white picket fence is what my first name is Du-En that's the first in the recipe all my children. That white picket fence was always the place where we recognize a beautiful family just cooling. LOVE, PEACE, and HAPPINESS is what we should be showing, and proving. Just like the Different Strokes show was doing. If they didn't have the internet then. We now would be ruined. Because now we would not know what we're doing. Look at the M.T. A now even in 2015 they're improving your riding on it now I know that was kinder confusing. On my birth certificate it reads Du-En capital D lowercase u DASH capital E lowercase n it spells Du-En peace all my children. PEACE.

· ·

By Du-En Rennie Foster Sr.
aka floetry poet

3   ☐6   ☐0   ☐TM   LY✊✊✊✊✍

360° FROM THE 70'S TO THE MILLENNIUM

floetry Rap.

The only thing that don't spin or change 360 Degrees backwards is time. 360 Degrees cipher is a circle, and that's the way the earth moves, and on 45's we heard our favorite grooves. We we're cutting up on Techiques Turn Tables, and spinning 360 degrees on our hands, head, and knees. The kids use to play with these spinning tops that was wood with a metal tip that helped it spin good, also a string came with it, you spin it like jerking a whip. Spin the bottle was my favorite, becuse thats the game you played with the finest chicks, you spin the bottle just to get a kiss, excuse me, and some times it went past the lips, and this is a solar eclipse when the moon revolves between the Earth, and the Sun.With a total eclipse this is how it's done the same way but the Sun is completely blocked out, and this is how the nine planets moved about, they revolved around the Sun 360 degrees with the same speed. Coney Island was the place to be, the Hell Whole was the ride for me, your body was stuck to the wall, and the floor drooped from below, and that wasn't it, the Himalyaya, and the Polar Express was cutting up every record moving so fast forward when your dancing on the outside looking in there on the outside but fenced in, and you can feel the wind from the the speed. When there moving 360 degrees, and when they stopped the DJ will say do you want to go backwards, and that was it my friend, and now to bring you up-to-date. The free weel spinners spinds while the BMW stays in place, and there's no more metal roller skates that stretches to your shoe sizewith a key, their roller blades yeppie! Even a new style is coming out check out what they got now NENO Sneakers there Tong has a twist it turns from White to Red with a flip of your wrist, it turns 360 degrees in 3 seconds. You might want to keep a record, and write this down, it's while now DVDs and CDs and GAME DISK have a consequence. So keep them fresh and moving at Their terrific speed in a motion of 360 degrees. You see they skip, I don't mean that they,skip from a scratch like the old vinyl or of waxed 45's, 78's, 33& a half. They skip literally forward, and back, and you can repeat any track. Now the vinyl didn't do that. That's the change in technology. The only thing that came close to that was the cassette tape, and the 8 track, and if you can remember that Old- T's Holla Back. Double-Dutch was PHAT 2 ropes turn individuality from the West to the East. POETRY in motion check out what the girls was dope in.

The girls use to just jump in the ropes while singing songs that came to mind, and made up their own rhymes, and freestyle with it, and black music was in the backround of it, from morning to night underneath the sidewalk street lights. Now to bring you up-to-date girls jumping Double-Dutch while doing the Harlem Shake, also Bush It Off. The girls never mess up at all. USHER, and LUDACRIS sing the song Yeah-Yeah. I guess by now you can guess what is 360 DEGRESS is about. Well lets see it's complete, and thats 360° from the 70's to the millennium. PEACE.

. . . .

By Du-En Rennie Foster Sr.
aka floetry poet

3 ☐6 ☐0 ☐™   LY☺☺☺☺◭

PRACTICE MAKES PERFECT

Love poem.

Lady you are the ultimate your mind can go to Infinity you don't have to increase your beauty, it's a symphony you look so buttery soft like your favorite leather jacket in the spring. You're not soft you work hard for everything. your respect comes naturally like new car technology radio, record player, 8-tracks, cassette tape, C.D, bluetooth, and now internet radio, done hit the car industry. Night, and day you're a QUEEN, you even wrote out your own philosophy. On why there's a light bulb on and it's over the heads of cartoons, and human beings. You're a true woman of loyalty. A real grade A of this Society. You would introduce how to compromise instantly for problem solving in relationships between man woman, and family when they're upset mad or angry you use a good methodology it's called common sense and affectionate thinking, described as a reasoning ability to work things out clearly. You understand organized cheering with soda, non-alcohol beverages or alcohol drinking chocolate candy or $100.00 for one plate of food that you love to sink your teeth in or you're in the kitchen cooking food that restaurants and you have an comparison in. At home practicing etiquette dinners after you had said your presidential campaign speeches and you still have time for your man and the family business, and outdoor camping on vacation weekends you practice whatever you're preaching I can go on for days so I'm going to get ready to add the word PEACE to this piece. I love you Ms. Heir's a CHEERS, and a KISS to HAPPINESS, and to bring about good well-rounded RELATIONSHIPS. PEACE equals Please Educate Allah's Children Everywhere and that's what you do my dear. PEACE.

. . . .

By Du-En Rennie Foster Sr.

aka floetry poet

3   ⬛6   ⬛D   ⬛™   LY🖐️🖐️🖐️🖐️✍️

MR. ABILITY
floetry Rap.

Mr. Ability the only one that I bow down to is Allah or God the most high Supreme Being no one who think that their Emperor or that they royalty or if there Minds can close the Seven Seas do you have the power to go back to the time when the doctors spanked breath into me? Are you a prime minister that's conquering the countries or an Ambassador that can overthrow the American Embassy? Are you a 5-star General and you want the world to salute thee? Do you have political powers holding down a whole democracy or maybe you can stop a tsunami? Are you my father, my sister, my brother, my mommy? Are you the president that can control the Marines, the Air Force, the Navy, the

Army?Can you control the zodiacs in the universe surroundings? Can you build the Pyramid better than the Egyptians did? Are you Immortal that you can make all four seasons just be Autumn? So Mr. Ability what type of mystery that you can be? That you don't bleed or use five senses just like me.You must think that you're the Son of Mary. You got's to be the Son of Mary messing with me. PEACE.

. . . .

By Du-En Rennie Foster Sr.
aka floetry poet

3　⬜6　⬜0　⬜™　LY✊✊✊✊✍

THEY DON'T STOP, TEARS ARE AROUND THE CLOCK

The Spoken Word.

My tears come out every hour, like the bird inside of a coo-coo clock also the sound that they makes is the sound of a teardrop, and I have a little toilet tissue left, and I'm back inside the S.H.U the Box aka special housing unit, soltary confinement. Sometimes I can see the light, and the ceiling or just the bottom of the top bunk so now my wax soaks up the tears that are almost used up, and I still can't hear the sound of a teardrop. But I do know the feelings that they got. The first second when a newborn baby in a delivery room starts, weddings, and times in the day, and in the dark, happy, and sad some are natural also some have mascara marks gangsters tattoo them on their faces a lot. Getting locked up, and going to KEEP LOCK if you did the crime or not, and funerals are always planned Around the Clock I wrote this while I was in the BOX.

PEACE.

. . . .

By Du-En Rennie Foster Sr.
aka floetry poet

3 ☐6 ☐0 ☐™ LY✊✊✊✊✍

TO THE ONE I LOVE TIGER CAT

Dedicated Love poem.

TIGER CAT my words are as light as a feather you can take one apart when you put this lesson together then in order to rebuild it you gots to be clever enough to go back to the knowledgement of a mind repair kit. TIGER CAT I can love you until cupids arrows in you no more they will stick. I'm a real grown man that will always have you always wanting it. Like to be able to read the paintings on the teepee tent. it's paintings are in Indian painting Graphics. TIGER CAT we would become tropical active, like when we were younger waiting for the fetus come out of the water and the Blackness. TIGER CAT I told Mr. Owl the world can't get the Sum to the center of this. How many licks does it take to get 360 individual love monments? Living the way of the Equator twice would be the size of it. If we were Adam and Eve the world be like back there Ms. it's would be so humongous our love making performance would be like this an arch of colors of red, green, blue and orange. We would be hot like the three bears when they're eating Porridge. Popeye eating his spinach can't stop us. We would be mentally, and physically challenged it will be so exotic. With the fireplace, the roses, and the chocolates, the music would be slow African, Korean, Spanish, and English. That would widen your mind radius, natural electricity will be the voltage you would need to turn sand into glass with this kind of speed 186 miles per second that's how fragile your heart is isn't it? TIGER CAT I will never break it or neglect it or put it into a total eclipse, your heartbeats 72 beats per second, like the red, and white blood cells I want to get up in it. TIGER CAT for you I got that fetish to bring about love, peace, and happiness. I want to take you to the Milky Way galaxy Ms. all the way to the last bottle of it. Now TIGER CAT I just THREE SIXTYED you something like a picture message texting do, and a video. TIGER CAT I'm coming to you like INTERNET radio. PEACE.

. . . .

By Du-En Rennie Foster Sr.
aka floetry poet

3   ☐6   ☐0   ☐TM   LY☺☺☺☺✑

FINALLY I'VE FOUND MY QUEEN

Dedicated Love poem.

TIGER CAT you look so good for this face-to-face distance, you make me want to use all 5 of my senses. A diamond is forever but my love for you is forever ever-ever witch makes my love for you 360 Degrees better. This is why I've aprouched you on August 24th 2019 Because your defanitions were like a magnet that brought me to you, and when you spoke your powerful mined did too boo I was estonish from looking, and listening to you, and you don't let your intelligences supperseed your Beauty you make them equally truly! You tell me this, and you tell me that you love for me is one hundred percent equality is that 100% you, and me or me, and you? So TIGER CAT does that sound familiar to YA' boo? You see when a man whispers sweet nothings in your ear that's all you will here, so TIGER CAT exhale my dear because I will tell you straight up babe I love you, and I truly care, and that would be face-to-face babe, and not in your ear. So when I get home from work tell me what is your nature of Services being requested in this atmosphere of love TIGER CAT I want us to be engaged in our love for hours, and years to come. So you see that's unconditional love. Girl you're one in a zillion your precious, and supreme your first impression left a notorious impression on me. That brought out my curiosity. PEACE.

. . . .

By Du-En Rennie Foster Sr.
aka floetry poet

3 ⬜6 ⬜0 ⬜™ LY😊😊😊😊✍

WHERE DO WE GO FROM HERE?

The Spoken Word.

Mankind can tell you an approximate time of when you'll be born, but can't tell you an approximate time of when your life is no MORE. It's written on paper and invisible form. It is rough here on Earth why would you still want it rough when your breath is gone? I'm coming up on the Rough Side of the Mountain is an impressive song. We can live our life 2 ways either right or wrong. I'm doing my best to make it in is the rest of the song. We're off to see the wizard what road was Dorothy on? The wizard had his people's reopen the doors like Doctor Martin Luther King Junior and Biggie Smalls, it was all a dream before it was a song Somewhere Over the Rainbow is where we live on PEACE.

. . . .

By Du-En Rennie Foster Sr.
aka floetry poet

3　☐6　☐0　☐™　LY🤜🤜🤜🤜✍

I CAN, BUT CAN YOU MAKE HEADS OR TELES OF THIS?

The Spoken Word.

I'm not blind to the ways of the modern humanbeing, a chisel, and a stone is not how my mind reads, and learning etiquettes, and the basic Foundations of The Facts of Life does not give me difficulties. Also rehearing my characteristics is not mind boggling. I'm a Libra I can get a good sense of balancing between right, and wrong, and my wants, and needs before the next fertilization of the embryo, and the fetus or baby gets released that process happens in 40 weeks. I had a dream of my own bobblehead of me. It was on my dresser reading my floetry. Then it told me your ingenious is developing. I'm bringing your present tense forward to where I be. Like a crystal ball in your mind I'm scanning your picture gallery like a smartphone of your newest technology. You'll be enhancing your journey in humanity just by saying your floetry at 360 Degrees PEACE.

. . . .

By Du-En Rennie Foster Sr.
aka floetry poet

3   ☐6   ☐0   ☐™   LY☺☺☺☺✍

TO MY GIRL TIGER CAT
Dedicated Love poem.

TIGER CAT my words are as light as a feather you can take one apart when you can put this lesson together then in order to rebuild it you got's to be clever enough to go back to the knowledgement of a mind repair kit. TIGER CAT I can love you until Cupids arrow's in you no more they will stick. I'm a real grown man that will always have you always wanting it. Like to be able to read the paintings on a teepee tent. It's paintings are in Indian paintings Graphics TIGER CAT we will become tropical active like when we were younger waiting for the fetus come out of the water and the Blackness. TIGER CAT I told Mr. Owl the world can't get the Sum to the center of this. How many licks does it take to get 360 individual love mon-ments? Living the way of the Equator twice would be the size, of it. TIGER CAT if we were Adam and Eve the world be like back thire Ms. it would be so humongous our love making performance would be like this an arch of Ms will be like this an arch of colors of red, green, blue, and orange. We would be hot like the Three Bears when they're eating porridge . Popeye eating his spinach can't stop us we will be mentally and physically challenged. It would be so exotic, with the fireplace, the roses, and the chocolates, the music would be slow African, Korean, Spanish, and English. That would widen your mind radius, natural electricity will be the voltage you will need to turn sand into glass with this kind of speed 186 miles per second that's how fragile your heart is isn't it? TIGER CAT I will never break it or neglect it or put it into a total eclipse, your heartbeat 72 beats per second like the red, and white blood cells I want to get up in it, TIGER CAT for you I got that fetish to bring about love, peace, and happiness. I want to take you to the Milky Way galaxy Ms. all the way to the last bottle of it. Now TIGER CAT I just THREE SIXTYED you something like a picture message texting do, and a video, I'm coming to you like internet radio. PEACE.

. . . .

By Du-En Rennie Foster Sr.
aka floetry poet

3   ☐6   ☐0   ☐™   LY✊✊✊✊✍

BASICALLY

Love poem.

Ma' you're my most popular chocolate like physically we both fit, when we're together no other couple can become a duplicate. Living as boyfriend, and girlfriend or as husband and wife is our environment, king and queen is what I really ment. In order to do this love must become the main ingredient. I'm always feeling you Ms. your beautiful like the sun rays on the earth after the rain has descendants a rainbow sometimes comes along with it. I love you my queen your so excellent the way you love me like McDonald's I'm loving it. We're in perfect sequence like the numbers and alphabets, and we stay in good tune like instruments babe you're sweet like Sunkist and if you don't remember they grow oranges. Darling you must be a hypnotist I'm glad our love is President that's first when you think of it. You got my nose open wider than the nostrils of a rhinoceros. This poem should have been called therapeutic. PEACE.

. . . .

By Du-En Rennie Foster Sr.
aka floetry poet

3   ☐6   ☐D   ☐™   LY☺☺☺☺✍

A MIXAPPEAL

Love poem.

Darling when the warm Blue Glare is coming from off of the water, and mixes with the yellow sun rays, it makes the water green and hoter along with a streak of lights, a rainbow underneath the water, like a highlighter magic marker. When we are together our love will build up a as 1 chemistry, that will cause us to not forget each other. Babe when we make love our passionate feelings will be so clever. That when we mix it it will make the fluids in, and on the outside of us mix directly together the name of the mixture we can Google it, and we still can't get the answer! PEACE.

. . . .

By Du-En Rennie Foster Sr.
aka floetry poet

3   ☐6   ☐0   ☐™   LY👊👊👊👊✍

I'M LAYING IT DOWN
floetry Rap.

Shakespeare, and shine a good POET's, and so am I, now it's my time to shine, I'm floetry POET 360 degrees, and I can say floetry faster than a hurricane blowing down trees because, I floe 360 degrees,I move faster than the A train moving with Express speed, and I'm slicker than the biggest man pushing weed, and collecting G's I'm floetry POET 360 degrees, and to the ladies you won't have me on Maury Povich saying 360 is the father of your baby. Maury would say 360 to baby X,Y,Z you're not the father and you will go through that dag-nab-it mama drama falling on your knees spinning 360 degrees, and saying Maury can I test another potential father please? Yes I'm a vet I'm talking about floetry terrorism because the Moon is next, I'm not talking about blowing it up. I want to blow out like Missy Elliott, Busta Rhymes, Erykah Badu, and Fat Joe, too. I'm so hot, and It's so hot in New York City all the women are smelling good, and looking pretty you have your girl, and I have mines, and me, and mines are rocking the PHAT shines, and we got on my own design clothing line, and my SAAB that I coped from Brooklyn East New York with the 21" Free Weel Spinners that I sport the only time that I walk is to pay for the gas.I have all kinds of credit card so I don't spend cash. I have my own FOSTER'S ON THE CHOW RESTARUNT SO my money will last, and on Saturday's I get on my John Deere rider so I can cut the grass, and clean out the pool, and sit back and read some vibe issues, and get on the 3way, and page my brother Vee, and the page would read floetry 360 degrees, and VON-AL knows that it's me. That's how I'm laying it DOWN!PEACE.

. . . .

By Du-En Rennie Foster Sr.

aka floetry poet

3　☐6　☐0　☐™　LY☻☻☻☻✍

SCIENTIFIC METHOD

Love poem.

Our X, and Y chromosomes when I was home is what acquainted us.

From when you were a embryo you grew to become compassionate. Your mind is beautiful you keep it so immaculate like The Golden Girls your heart is true, I love the way you fashioned it. If you was able to send me a text message I would text message, I would text you back, it would read to my love thanks for sending that text. I love you two better than floetry that I do the best. Now, and before all these years I love the way you have represented, I know when you get home from after our prison visit your exhaling from that long day for about 120 minutes. Then the phone rings, and your heart, and soul has no Calamity in it. You know it's me calling you 4 hours later right after our visit thank you for all the ways you have taken care of me I would never forget it I love you and I'll see you on my next visit, and that's not a SCICNTIFIC METHOD. PEACE.

- -

By Du-En Rennie Foster Sr.

aka floetry poet

3   6   0   TM   LY

AFTER THIS MESSAGE YOUR HEART WILL BE RIGHT BACK

floetry Rap.

I would take your foundation right from underneath your feet, and place acupunctur needles inside your brain, and that would make your mind sleep. I'm the puppet master of 2015. Like Pinochio I don't want to use any string. I want to be a real boy is the song that you would sing. No push-to-start buttons like on the march of the Wooden Soldiers, with Laurel, and Hardy. I will control you with the same technology that was used to build virtual reality. I would have you walking around in the shape of geometry In each shape separately, mathematically they equal 360 degrees. I've been in general population, S.H.U, keep lock the why me pin, 200 S. Block, I.C.U, and B.H.U. Bipolar 2, and ADHD are my intellectual disabilitys.They are not interventions they are like the chickens that come home to roost that means customarily they are a Natural Geographic Inside my mind's body. They spread like in EBOLA so their quarantine inside me. This is an analysis of your HEART BEAT when you were listening to what my brain had my VOICE BOX SPEAK. It Skipped as your mind thought what was the words that Ms. Tiana Gardner speaks. Now just think of the song in your mine, and put it on repeat thank you Ms. Tiana Gardner for singing the song HEART BEAT. PEACE.

By Du-En Rennie Foster Sr.

aka floetry port

3 ⬛6 ⬛0 ⬛™ LY😊😊😊😊✍

MS. K. THE CASE WORKER

Dedicated floetry poem.

This is a dedication floetry poem to Ms. K. If you ask me Ms. K. is a good case worker with a good personality, she deals with your needs that requires responsibilities. A lot of times she will go out of her way just to see you or me. With out invasion of our privacy, but if that's what you talking about then Ms. K. is listening. As long as it's not disrespecting. She tries her very best to get us out of the shelter Community, sometimes it can be a long or short while, while her computer is processing, because it's over 500 men in the Keener building. THANK YOU

Ms.K. for all of your HELP. PEACE. By Du-En Rennie Foster Sr. aka floetry poet 360 date 12. 10. 2019

. . . .

By Du-En Foster Sr.
aka floetry poet

3   ☐6   ☐0   ☐™   LY☺☺☺☺✍

MERRY CHRISTMAS TO MY FRIEND NICOLA

Dedicated floetry poem.

Merry Christmas to a woman with a beautiful heart. Nicola you, and I kept a good work relationship from the very start. Even if I get a nine-to-five my memories of you will never depart. You're like the joy of Christmas that's why wrote this poem to you with all my heart. Also all I brought from you was a hat and a scarf I will put it underneath the Christmas tree with the rest of the presents that my family got. By the way my daughter loves the hat and scarf a lot. This is what Santa elf's are singing in their toy shop. Sleigh bells ringing Nicola are you listening? We're singing along to the C.D's Christmas songs, on a Downtown Brooklyn Wonderland, and maybe together we can build a snow woman, and dress her up with hats and scarves, and branches from pine trees, and watch all the children eye light up with glee, You'll say hi, I'll say hi, then we'll wave again I'll see you on Kwanzaa morning around 10. At that time it would be work again. Then once again I can wave at my good friend.Nicola Merry Christmas to you and your family, and Happy New Year PEACE.

. . . .

By Du-En Rennie Foster sr.

aka floerty poet

3   ☐6   ☐0   ☐TM   LY🖐🖐🖐🖐✍

TIGER CAT & FLOETRY
POET 3 ⬜6 ⬜0 ⬜

Dedicated Love floetry poem.

TIGER CAT you bring out the best in me. 360 is my recipe.That will have you purring120 x 3. Now in your 3rd. eye do your math with me. That equals a good relationship triangle that's 360. TIGER CAT that's how you inspire me. We are each other's highest elevation of EQUALITY your BEAUTY is a reality dream virtual reality is not for you and me. Our love, and love-making is the real dag-nab-it thing. We don't have to Google on how to present ourselves as KING, and QUEEN I compliment you on everything, and in return you do the same thing. We love saying poetry, and floetry at the PEACE CAFE'. Also on the bus, and on the train we've kissed, talked, laugh, and with each other we've danced, and to each other we sang. We even took a walk in the park with YING-YANG. Walking with a dog is a wonderful thing. Especially when it's winter and it feels like a spring day. You're awesome, in each, and every way you're not a voodoo woman but you shape my heart, my mind, my body, my soul as if it was clay. Also I'm not a puppet master because you don't move you that way. But I do move you the gentleman's way. Helping you with your coat when we're entering or leaving a place.Opening doors, making sure you're safe. Making sure you're walking on the proper side of me. Giving you a umbrella to protect you from the rain, snow or heat. At home or in a restaurant I'll pull up your seat. Listening to you as you speak. Kissing you goodnight, and saying goodnight before we go to sleep, and in the morning together thanking the lord before we even eat. We love it when we call each other SWEETIE PIE because to each other we are so sweet. That's 90 x 4 = 360 so that's a square PEACE, and I'm not a square by any means. Thank you for being with me you're pretty like the Tiger Lillies but the CIPHER isn't complete. TIGER CAT I love you because you are the woman that keep our minds at peace. Ever since I've met you we've never had a argument but we had 2 debates we are finally in an excellent relationship that makes our past relationships with other men, and women Bull-Mess has finally come to a cease. I floetry poet 360 assure you TIGER CAT that those bad relationships that we both has been in FOR US WILL NOT BE A REPEAT .So 180 + 180 equals 360 which makes this poetry, floetry poem almost circular complete. TIGER CAT, MY SWEETIE PIE I LOVE YOU. I had to put that on repeat.Now this poetry, floetry poem is circular complete. PEACE.

· ·

By Du-En Rennie Foster Sr.
aka floetry poet

3   ☐6   ☐0   ☐™   LY☺☺☺☺✍

WITH POETRY I FLOEMULATED MY POEM WITH A SONG

Dedcated Love floetry poem.

TIGER CAT, why I love you so much? Monica really brought that question up. Because like India Arie you have a steady love. You're the one that I'm always thinking of. With a Empire State of Mind Alicia Keys, and Jay-Z. The Temptations Treat Her Like a Lady. Just because you're the highest entity. Among the Lord fluently, like the Nefertiti, by me you'll always be loved phenomenally. I'm Hopelessly Devoted to you. By Olivia Newton John. Like the Barry White song. I can't Get Enough of your love in a substantial loving way you're driving me 360° crazy. Like the words of The Beatles

You Really Got a Hold on Me Babe. Your Honey Love is fascinating. R-Kelly dedicated Honey Love to all the ladies. Fascinating I'm dedicating to you babe. Like The Gap Band your outstanding. Like Vice President Elect-Kamala Harris, and President-Elect Joe Biden. TIGER CAT, like Teddy Pendergrass said you're my latest, and you're my greatest, my latest, my greatest inspiration. You inspired me to do my Poetry more than my mind can process to scribe some new floetry. TIGER CAT, so like Jodeci come, and talk to me? About the confidence of your mind that I can view but I can't see, and living a life as Catherine which means Pure added on to Purity. TIGER CAT, thanks for being with me, in a relationship that is already 360 with a few defects of character. TIGER CAT, can you explain the answer 99.9% is what the relationship equal. A perfect relationship will be the sequel. Hint-Hint we will be in it in the future surrounded by a lot of people. By Next will you be my wifey? Yes I'll be your wifey sweetie pie I love thee. PEACE.

· ·

By Du-En Rennie Foster Sr.

aka floetry poet

3　☐6　☐D　☐TM　LY☺☺☺☺✐

WORD!
The Spoken Word.

I'm taking my mind to reform school. A metamophosis is what I put my mind through. Something like what a caterpillar do in a cocoon.The outcome is so beautiful. Also I'll change my movements that what a real human being do. Then I'll reformulate my mannerism, and characteristics too. I'll be thinking which will articulate my social skills, and social speaking then I'll have effective communication. So when I say my floetry you can understand what I'm saying. Each one of my sentences have common sense, and knowledge, and wisdom but you can't understand them if you're not listening. Not just with your ears but with your imagination. Your heart has its own destination. A verbal puzzle is what I'm saying! Staying well-rounded that's the kind of person to you I'm bringing. Proactive is how I'm proceeding, to climb with Minds like Minds have meanings. Even if you have a mental disability like ADHD like me. No segregation between intellectual thinking. Now my Libra has cell phone, and Smartwatch, Syncing. Also I promise 99.9% there's no Dr. Jekyll, and Mr. Hyde Gene separation in me. PEACE.

· ·

By Du-En Rennie Foster Sr.
aka floetry poet

3 ☐6 ☐0 ☐™   LY☺☺☺☺✍

AFRICAN AMERICAN RECONSTRUCTION INSTRUCTIONS

The Spoken Word.

I'm thinking outside of the box. That's the box that is already outside of the box. That's the box that is before the box, that is out side of the box. That's the box that is outside in the rain. Like the Muslims that follow the most honorable Elijah Muhammad say Make It plain. Check out the technology knowledge that I am writing,and saying. The cleansing is from the rain in our mind makes a correction I'm not playing. It's like rebooting your Wi-Fi router connection. Then you can learn how to pair your smart watch Bluetooth voice in your smartphone child or children direction.

REMEMBER if @ first you don't succeed try, try again. If at first your Bluetooth voice has a bad connection then go to troubleshooting. Reread your minds good parenting directions. Find out what's wrong with the child or children then you find out what how to step in now you can have a verbal and listening conversation you can sit back and listen to what your child or children is saying. Don't say anything just nod your head and squint your eyebrows to they're complaining. You need to use listening discipline. Let the child or children finished talking, and thinking. Then you can interject to them. If that doesn't work and go to a smartphone and Smartwatch number syncing. See what you'll have compatible in thinking. This is mostly for a preteen, and teen observation.

If that doesn't work then go to a religion. You study a few religions like a new blind man or woman study cooking in the kitchen. Depends on their age let them pick out the religion, that they fit in. Now you got a network connection now the smartphone, and Smartwatch will stay connected as long as you pay your phone bill every minute. Now you're ready for some old-fashioned discipline business keep it Culture African-American. That's our ethnic we should be practicing it. Also using nonviolent as a punishment social science the scientific study of human society, and social relationships when you use your Google Assistant, so your mind can kick in on a different wavelengths. It will be a piece of cake. Now you can have a better metime for yourself so you can think, about the punishment you about to make. Also teaching, and training your child or children to obey rules regulation, and practice their behavior for goodness sake so we can properly calibrate. PEACE.

. . . .

By Du-En Rennie Foster Sr.
aka floetry poet

3   ☐6   ☐D   ☐™   LY✊✊✊✊✍

NEW CHAPTER

Dedicated Love floetry poem.

I know the difference between the 3 phases HAPPY BIRTHDAY, TIGER CAT you're the first woman I've ever fell in LOVE with in the correct time that it was 360 Degrees that made it to be 99.9% perfect. No shotgun wedding because she got pregnant also I fell in love as the time went. I even got married in the spirit of the moment. Because I was high, and drunk, and for the second time there was No engagement but to you Catherine Keith a engagement ring I had to present. Wedding Bells Are Ringing that's the NEXT STEP. TIGER CAT not to Pat ourselves on the back but for us that's how we represent. Thank you TIGER CAT on December 31st 2020 saying yesssss! As for that we are blessed I love you TIGER CAT you're the Best. HAPPY BIRTHDAY. I'll be right back with Poetry with a floe. TWO

. . . .

By Du-En Rennie Foster Sr.
Aka floetry poet 360

PEACE.
4/18/2021

ORDER FORM

| Qty | Check One | | | Please Print | Unit Price | Total Price |
	Audio	Video	Book	Title		

Name_____

Address _____

City/State/Zip _____

Phone _____

SUBTOTAL	
SHIPPING	
TOTAL	

Check one: VISA ☐   MASTERCARD ☐   Exp. Date: _____